YEARS A, B, & C

Mindful
Meditations

for
***Every Day
of Lent***
and
Easter

Rev. Warren J. Savage

———❧———

Mary Ann McSweeny

Liguori
ONE LIGUORI DRIVE
LIGUORI MO 63057-9999

Imprimi Potest: Thomas D. Picton, CSsR
Provincial, Denver Province, The Redemptorists

Published by Liguori Publications
Liguori, Missouri 63057
To order, call 800-325-9521, or visit www.liguori.org.

Library of Congress Cataloging-in-Publication Data

Savage, Warren J.
  Mindful meditations for every day of Lent and Easter : years A, B, and
C / Warren J. Savage, Mary Ann McSweeny.—1st ed.
      p. cm.
  ISBN 978-0-7648-1969-8
  1. Lent—Prayers and devotions. 2. Easter—Prayers and devotions.
3. Catholic Church—Prayers and devotions. 4. Catholic Church.
Lectionary for Mass (U.S.) 5. Bible—Devotional literature. I.
McSweeny, Mary Ann. II. Title.
  BX2170.L4S28 2011
  242'.34—dc22

                                                          2010030792

Printed in the United States of America
15 14 13 12 11 / 6 5 4 3 2
First edition

Contents

Introduction

During the annual season of Lent, the universal church is invited to turn away from sin and be faithful to the gospel. It is a time of personal reflection and inner, spiritual renewal, of fasting, prayer, and almsgiving; of conversion of heart; of mutual forgiveness and love; of compassion; of peace and reconciliation; of the call to holiness.

Lent is a time we set aside to enter into our own personal desert to confront the demons and obstacles that prevent us from being faithful followers of Christ. It is a time to reflect on the meaning of our Christian human existence. It is a time to shed our false images and notions of who we are. It is a time to place God at the center of our lives. It is a time of self-examination that leads to a change of heart.

This book poses a challenge in a culture that encourages us to spend our time, energy, and resources satisfying our own desires and interests rather than looking out for the needs and concerns of others. Living Lent with an attentive, caring heart will demand a large measure of personal commitment, perseverance, and discipline.

The goal is not to get through Lent but to live

Lent with the awareness of our dependence upon God and the constant need to discern the will of God in our daily works. Embracing these daily readings, reflections, prayers, and practices will help us to purify our hearts, control our desires, and serve the Lord in freedom.

On the day of Easter, may we be a better people and have a better disposition of heart to share with others and live out in our lives the risen Lord's transforming message of love, compassion, and peace.

Ash Wednesday

Joel 2:12–18
Psalm 51:3–4, 5–6ab, 12–13, 14, 17
2 Corinthians 5:20—6:2
Matthew 6:1–6, 16–18

Create in me a clean heart, O God, and put a new and right spirit within me.

PSALM 51:10

Reflection: Once a year we need to get a physical examination to make sure we are healthy. Once a year we are supposed to get our teeth cleaned. It is recommended that every three to five thousand miles we should change the oil and filter in our cars and rotate the tires.

Most people wake up each day, refresh their bodies with a shower or bath, put on clean clothes, and face the challenges of the day. Some people treat themselves to a wonderful body massage, a nice manicure, and a pedicure. Others register at a health fitness center to exercise their bodies, getting advice from a trainer on how to stay toned and in shape. There seems to be a great deal of focus and concentration on outward physical appearances. Do we give as much attention and care to our inner, spiritual life?

Taking care of our bodies is very important, but taking care of our heart and soul is perhaps more important because our true nature comes from within us. Lent is a time for us to examine our inner life and our hearts, where the true self resides. It is a time to check in on our relationship with God. It is a time for us to take a deeper look at the things that impede our ability to show love, care, compassion, mercy, and forgiveness to others. Lent is the time to ask God to help us to create a clean heart and reorder our lives with a right spirit, a steadfast spirit of love and concern for the whole world.

Ponder: What do I plan to work on during Lent?

Prayer: Lord, create in me a clean heart and instill within me your spirit of love and peace.

Practice: Today I will pray for a change of heart; I will fast from being narcissistic; I will make time for personal prayer and meditation.

Thursday After Ash Wednesday

Deuteronomy 30:15–20
Psalm 1:1–2, 3, 4, 6
Luke 9:22–25

"If any want to become my followers, let them deny themselves and take up their cross daily and follow me."

LUKE 9:23

Reflection: Before we begin to do our inner work, we need to dethrone ourselves from being the center of the world. We are so used to being self-centered, self-focused, or self-absorbed. The only person we see is the one standing in the center. In the early days of Lent, we are challenged to let go of being in control, of wanting all the attention, and of seeking after short-term relief from our unhappiness with ourselves and life.

When we allow God to be the center of our lives, we are able to see ourselves in a different light. In God's light we can see our inner beauty and goodness. We can see that being in right relationship with God keeps us happy and whole. Our daily cross or struggle is staying in right relationship with God. There are many voices coming into our heads telling us that we don't need God. There are strong forces all around us enticing us with material things and promises of wealth, power, and control to make ourselves the center of the world.

It is not easy to be a follower of the humble Christ, who calls us to let go of everything so that we can find our true humanity and true happiness. As the journey of Lent begins, we are invited to let Christ be the center of our world and to sit in the light of his Word, seeking wisdom for the days ahead.

Ponder: What is my daily cross?

Prayer: Lord, you are the center of my life. Give me a trusting heart to remain faithful to you and myself in times of self-doubt and personal struggles.

Practice: Today I will pray for a spirit of trust; I will fast from self-doubt; I will dedicate some of my time and resources to a project for the poor.

Friday After Ash Wednesday

Isaiah 58:1–9a
Psalm 51:3–4, 5–6ab, 18–19
Matthew 9:14–15

Is not this the fast that I choose: to loose the bonds of injustice, to undo the thongs of the yoke, to let the oppressed go free, and to break every yoke? Is it not to share your bread with the hungry, and bring the homeless poor into your house; when you see the naked, to cover them, and not to hide yourself from your own kin?

ISAIAH 58:6–7

Reflection: Our lives move at express-train speed, passing by all the problems of the world, without time to reflect on how we are all connected and need to help one another. There are many public prophets calling our attention to the needs of others, but we choose to hide ourselves from our own; we refuse to tap into the wellspring of God's mercy and compassion in our hearts. Lent is a time to listen to the voices of prophets around us, the ones dedicated to doing the works of mercy not for self-recognition, but for the sake of God and the good of humanity. God does not expect us to be the saviors, but God does desire that we do what is right, good, and just, that we feed the hungry, clothe the naked, shelter the homeless, visit the sick and incarcerated, and show the mercy and compassion of God to all people. Through these acts of mercy and compassion, we show others what it means to be in right relationship with God and our neighbor.

Ponder: How do I show God's mercy and compassion to others?

Prayer: Lord, you are the mercy and compassion of God in the world. Soften my heart to be more sensitive to the needs of others.

Practice: Today I will pray for mercy and compassion; I will fast from being inconsiderate; I will commit to doing a work of mercy.

Saturday After Ash Wednesday

Isaiah 58:9b–14
Psalm 86:1–2, 3–4, 5–6
Luke 5:27–32

[Jesus] went out and saw a tax collector named Levi, sitting at the tax booth; and he said to him, "Follow me." And he got up, left everything, and followed him.

LUKE 5:27

Reflection: Levi is completely consumed by his work as a tax collector; sitting at the tax booth defines his existence and purpose in life. Levi is a symbol of someone who is "attached" or "joined" to something that gives him or her a sense of security and purpose in life. In general, most of us are preoccupied with something. We are attached to things and situations that consume our attention and give us a sense of security, purpose, and delight. Lent presents us with another important challenge: to examine our attachments in life. Are we so "attached" or "joined" to the things of this world that we have no time, space, or ability to be with the triune God? Levi must have re-examined his life and decided to detach himself from the tax booth and everything else that consumed his life to be with Jesus. Following Jesus demands personal sacrifice and detachment from things and situations that paralyze our ability to follow Jesus with all our mind, heart, soul, and strength. Jesus still walks toward us, sees us preoccupied with something, and offers us an invitation: "Follow me."

Ponder: What am I afraid to let go of to follow Jesus?

Prayer: Lord, you call me by name and invite me to be your disciple. Give me a courageous heart to leave everything and follow you.

Practice: Today I will pray for strength; I will fast from fear; I will make a personal inventory and give up something for Lent.

First Sunday of Lent

YEAR A

Genesis 2:7–9; 3:1–7
Psalm 51:3–4, 5–6, 12–13, 17
Romans 5:12–19
Matthew 4:1–11

Then the LORD God formed man from the dust of the ground, and breathed into his nostrils the breath of life; and the man became a living being.

GENESIS 2:7

Reflection: Life would be so much easier if we did not try to rewrite the story and play the part of God, pretending that we are the ones who control the universe, and can do whatever we like with this life, taking all matters into our own hands. How easy it is to forget that the "breath of life" is a gift from God given to every living creature on this earth. It was God's plan in the beginning that every living being be connected by the breath of love, peace, and compassion. God's "breath of life" created a communion of life and a universal family of people from different races, traditions, cultures, social backgrounds, and ways of life.

In our unawareness, we can be tempted to disregard the truth that every living being breathes in and out the divine life of God, and to show a lack of concern for others by our words and actions. Wherever the journey of life takes us, we must remember that we were created to be humble servants of God and to breathe out love, peace, and compassion into the world.

Ponder: How do I enhance or diminish the gift of life from God?

Prayer: Lord, deepen my awareness of and respect for your presence in creation and in the people around me.

Practice: Today I will pray for a deeper love and respect for life; I will fast from self-righteousness; I will offer my time, talent, and treasure to a local organization that provides help to the poor and needy.

Year B

Genesis 9:8–15
Psalm 25:4–5, 6–7, 8–9
1 Peter 3:18–22
Mark 1:12–15

God said, "This is the sign of the covenant that I make between me and you and every living creature that is with you, for all future generations. I have set my bow in the clouds, and it shall be a sign of the covenant between me and the earth."

GENESIS 9:12–13

Reflection: God takes the initiative to enter into a covenant with humanity, with every living creature, and with the earth. In this covenant, God promises to be faithful to us, love us, watch over us, and care for us. In this covenant, we promise to be faithful, loving partners with God. The covenant simply reminds us that we are always in relationship with God, each other, and the earth.

We break covenant when we ignore our relationship with God and try to make progress in life without acknowledging God as the source and foundation of our lives. We break covenant when we refuse to love our brothers and sisters and show compassion to those who are poor, oppressed, suffering, and in pain. We break covenant when we exploit the resources of the earth to satisfy our greedy tendencies, pollute the air and water, and destroy the environment.

It is time to take another look at the covenant we have with God, with humanity, and with the earth. It is time for us to recommit as an individual and a community to spending quality time with God in prayer and meditation, to being more compassionate to the needs and concerns of others, and to being more attentive to the ways we use the earth and its resources.

Ponder: What does it mean to live a covenantal life?

Prayer: Lord, strengthen my resolve to be faithful to your covenant of love and be more compassionate and generous toward all people.

Practice: Today I will pray for understanding; I will fast from selfishness and self-centeredness; I will spend time doing community service and advocating for care for creation.

Year C

Deuteronomy 26:4–10
Psalm 91:1–2, 10–11, 12–13, 14–15
Romans 10:8–13
Luke 4:1–13

When the Egyptians treated us harshly and afflicted us by imposing hard labor on us, we cried to the LORD, the God of our ancestors; the LORD heard our voice and saw our affliction, our toil, and our oppression.

DEUTERONOMY 26:6–7

Reflection: From the beginning of time, human beings have hurt other human beings by taking advantage of the weak. Throughout human civilization, individuals, and groups of people have been deaf to the cry of the poor, blind to the evil of slavery, and detached from the pain and suffering inflicted by others. Who will hear the voices of the men, women, and children from all over the globe who are forced into unpaid labor, sexual servitude, or coerced prostitution? An estimated 800,000 to 900,000 people worldwide each year fall victim to human trafficking, the new slavery of the twenty-first century.

No one is created to be exploited or taken advantage of because of deplorable living conditions. As children of God, we have an obligation to defend the dignity of every human person and seek ways to protect innocent victims from inhumane practices such as human trafficking. We are the presence of God's compassion in the world today.

Just as God heard the voices of the Israelites in Egypt—a place of slavery and oppression—and saw their suffering, their forced labor, and oppression, we, too, must hear the voices of the people who are recruited, transported, transferred, and harbored for the purpose of exploitation.

Ponder: How do I become an advocate for human rights?

Prayer: Lord, give me the courage to accept the painful, ugly realities of life and become your advocate of truth and justice in the world.

Practice: Today I will pray for a sense of justice; I will fast from complacency; I will become familiar with options for charity and advocacy regarding the trafficking of persons.

First Week of Lent

MONDAY

Leviticus 19:1–2, 11–18
Psalm 19:8, 9, 10, 15
Matthew 25:31–46

I have given you as a covenant to the people, a light to the nations.

Reflection: We often shine our light of kindness and love without conscious effort: giving directions to a visitor, preparing a nutritious meal for our family, offering condolences to a grieving person. At other times we have to overcome our tendency to be self-centered in order to let our light shine: speaking respectfully to someone who has been discourteous to us, giving up free time to help someone in need, choosing to be grateful even when things don't go our way.

The work of shining our light in the world is important. We help sustain faith in God's care and compassion when we show care and compassion to others. We keep hope alive when we comfort those who are suffering. We spread peace and joy when our life example shows others we are living with love as our center and purpose.

God has given each of us life so that we may be a light to all as we live out the covenant of God's love. It is humbling to realize that we are each an essential part of God's vision for the world: to establish justice for all who are oppressed and victimized; to open the eyes of those who are blind to goodness and generosity; to free prisoners of greed and fear; to make God's spirit of love and peace felt wherever people live.

Ponder: How do I shine my light in the world?

Prayer: Lord, you have filled me with your Spirit of love and goodness. Lead me out of the darkness of selfishness that I may be a light of faith, hope, and love to my sisters and brothers in need.

Practice: Today I will pray to be filled with love and compassion; I will fast from self-absorption; I will make all of my conversations opportunities to speak positively and with hope.

First Week of Lent

TUESDAY

Isaiah 55:10–11
Psalm 34:4–5, 6–7, 16–17, 18–19
Matthew 6:7–15

I sought the LORD, and he answered me, and delivered me from all my fears.

PSALM 34:4

Reflection: The habit of fear takes a lot of energy and becomes an ingrained, unhealthy, meaningless way of life. We fear not having any friends. We fear unemployment. We fear our boss. We fear being rejected. We fear failure. We fear success. We fear going hungry. We fear not having the right clothes. We fear strangers. We fear we might not be able to meet our mortgage payments. We fear our identities may be stolen. We fear the next generation will stop going to church. We fear terrorist attacks. We fear illness. We fear growing old. We fear death. We fear we are unlovable.

We have the illusion of being in control when we worry and fret and put our focus on what might go wrong. We think we are preparing ourselves for any eventuality, but we are really wearing down our inner resources and becoming spiritually, mentally, emotionally, and physically depleted.

Fear is the problem. Seeking God is the solution. With God we find faith that gives us the strength to face every problem that surfaces. With God we find hope that leads us to see goodness and beauty wherever we look. With God we find unconditional love that helps us to let go of fear and live in joy.

Ponder: What fears do I need to release to God?

Prayer: Lord, you are the source of love and life. Help me to seek you when I am afraid. Remove my fears that I may live in peace with my neighbors.

Practice: Today I will pray for faith in God's love and care; I will fast from fear; I will pray the "Our Father."

First Week of Lent

WEDNESDAY

Jonah 3:1–10
Psalm 51:3–4, 12–13, 18–19
Luke 11:29–32

And the people of Ninevah believed God; they proclaimed a fast, and everyone, great and small, put on sackcloth.

JONAH 3:5

Reflection: There are moments in life when we look reality in the face and finally believe what we see. We see the reality of a loved one's addiction. We see the reality of a dead-end job. We see the reality of the ways we have tried to manipulate and control others. We see the reality of the harm we have done to ourselves and others through our lack of respect and love.

God's commandment to love our neighbors as ourselves is truly what God requires of us. At every level of society, all people need to believe that.

All of us—from government officials to church leaders to business executives to workers to families—need to examine our lives. We need to accept the reality that we have sometimes acted in ways that are contrary to the law of love. We need to find the courage to admit our failures and wear the sackcloth of contrition.

For all of us, asking for God's forgiveness and guidance opens us to a new life in God. Entrusting our lives to God's tender care means we are willing to be reformed into an even greater image of God's goodness and love.

Ponder: What reality do I need to accept?

Prayer: Lord, you are the source of compassion and mercy. Give me a humble, contrite heart that I may believe in your goodness and love and entrust my life to your care.

Practice: Today I will pray for the willingness to practice God's command to love; I will fast from denial; I will examine my conscience to discover where I need to make changes in how I treat others.

First Week of Lent

THURSDAY

Esther C:12, 14–16, 23–25 (NAB)
Psalm 138:1–2ab, 2cde–3, 7c–8
Matthew 7:7–12

[Jesus taught them, saying:] "In everything do to others as you would have them do to you."

MATTHEW 7:12

Reflection: When things go wrong, we have a tendency to point the finger of blame at others and complain about how we are being treated. We use up precious mental and emotional resources imagining how life would be if others would only act differently. Yet, we cannot control others. We cannot change their thoughts, words, behaviors, or actions. We can only make a difference by changing ourselves. We can begin the work of love by deciding how we want to be treated and set an example by our own practice.

If we want respect, we show respect. If we want

gratitude, we practice gratitude. If we want to be encouraged, we offer encouragement. If we want to be heard, we listen. If we want to be spoken to with courtesy, we speak courteously. If we want friendship, we learn to be a good friend. If we want help, we give help. If we want to feel welcome, we welcome others. If we want to be loved, we love.

God gives us plenty of support as we do our best to love our neighbors as ourselves. Not only has God sent the Holy Spirit to fill us and guide us, but also Jesus offers us a concrete rule to live by: We are to treat others as we wish to be treated.

Ponder: How do I treat others?

Prayer: Lord, you answer when I call for help. Help me to put your golden rule into practice that I may be a source of healing and love for others.

Practice: Today I will pray to be mindful of others' needs; I will fast from blaming others; I will treat others as I wish to be treated.

First Week of Lent

FRIDAY

Ezekiel 18:21–28
Psalm 130:1–2, 3–4, 5–7a, 7bc–8
Matthew 5:20–26

[Jesus taught them, saying:] "But I say to you that if you are angry with a brother or sister, you will be liable to judgment."

MATTHEW 5:22

Reflection: Anger is an emotion that can arise for a variety of reasons. Perhaps our expectations aren't met. Perhaps someone misuses us. Perhaps our integrity is questioned. Perhaps we witness an injustice. Yet, feeling anger often makes us uncomfortable. We may judge ourselves as bad because we feel the anger. We may think that a good, loving person would never feel angry.

In our haste to stop the uncomfortable feeling of anger, we often act on it. We hold a grudge, sit in judgment, seek revenge, spread malicious gossip, speak sarcastically, or become depressed. When we act out in anger, we create even more layers of discomfort and guilt, and we may cause irreparable harm.

If we are able to accept anger as a part of the human condition, we will stop judging ourselves for feeling it and will no longer need to push anger away, deny it, suppress it, or act on it. We will find that we forgive ourselves and our sisters and brothers more easily when we accept that we all feel the human emotions of anger, sadness, fear, and joy. When we understand that all people—including ourselves—are in need of mercy, love, and compassion, we will find that the anger that arises in us also passes quickly.

Ponder: How do I respond to anger?

Prayer: Lord, with you there is kindness and redemption. Forgive me for judging myself and others. Help me to accept the fullness of the human experience, including uncomfortable feelings such as anger.

Practice: Today I will pray to accept myself and others just as we are; I will fast from judging my emotions; I will let go of a grudge I have been holding.

First Week of Lent

SATURDAY

Deuteronomy 26:16–19
Psalm 119:1–2, 4–5, 7–8
Matthew 5:43–48

[Jesus taught them, saying:] "Love your enemies and pray for those who persecute you."

MATTHEW 5:44

Reflection: When we feel vulnerable, we do not always remember God's command to love. Yet there is no compromise in Jesus' teaching to love our enemies. Love is the universal moral code by which we must live.

Love doesn't mean we don't set boundaries. It doesn't mean we can't protect ourselves. It doesn't mean we tolerate unacceptable behavior.

Love means seeking peaceful solutions to problems. It means humbly acknowledging our mistakes and changing our ways. It means dialoguing rather than dictating. It means giving a voice to all people and listening to others' opinions. It means responding with respect to the needs of others. It means refraining from doing harm. It means honoring the image of God's goodness and love in all people.

When we feel persecuted, we need to remember that behind the persecution is a person in need of mercy, compassion, and forgiveness. We need to examine our own lives to see where we have persecuted others. We need to be willing to pray for those who hurt us and those we have hurt. Prayer opens our hearts to God's healing power and brings about positive change.

Ponder: Have I led a blameless life?

Prayer: Lord, you are the source of love and peace. Soften my heart that I may learn to love those who have hurt me.

Practice: Today I will pray for a spirit of peace and forgiveness; I will fast from criticizing others; I will ask God to bless someone who is persecuting me.

Second Sunday of Lent

YEAR A

_____

Genesis 12:1–4a
Psalm 33:4–5, 18–19, 20, 22
2 Timothy 1:8b–10
Matthew 17:1–9

While he was still speaking, suddenly a bright cloud overshadowed them, and from the cloud a voice said, "This is my Son, the Beloved; with him I am well pleased; listen to him!"

MATTHEW 17:5

Reflection: God is still speaking to us, but are we listening? God gives us what we need to live a healthy spiritual life amid personal pain and suffering. God speaks to us each day in the beauty of creation, reminding us of the truth: we are part of God's mysterious plan and vision. We need to pay closer attention to our natural environment and be more mindful of the presence of God in nature around us. We will be able to live a more peaceful and contemplative life. God also speaks to us in the Word of God. When we read and meditate on the Word of God, we come to know Jesus, his message, and mission on a deeper level. God invites us to listen to Jesus in the Word of God. The Word of God, "the bright cloud" that overshadows the Christian life, speaks words of love, compassion, forgiveness, and peace to us. To love means to listen with an attentive heart. When we read the Word of God to listen to the voice of God, we show the depth of our love for God and our neighbor.

Ponder: How much time do I spend reading the Word of God, listening to the voice of God?

Prayer: Lord, open my ears to hear your invitation to listen to your Son in the Word of God and my heart to discern what it means to be your humble servant.

Practice: Today I will pray for a spirit of discernment; I will fast from procrastination; I will find time to join a Bible study group.

YEAR B

Genesis 22:1–2, 9a, 10–13, 15–18
Psalm 116:10, 15, 16–17, 18–19
Romans 8:31b–34
Mark 9:2–10

"Do not lay your hand on the boy or do any-thing to him; for now I know that you fear God, since you have not withheld your son, your only son, from me."

GENESIS 22:12

Reflection: The child is often a symbol of human weakness and helplessness. Many children worldwide are left homeless, poor, and vulnerable because of natural disasters, poverty, genocide, violence, and war. In this passage we hear and feel the heart of God through the voice of a messenger, "Do not lay your hand on the boy or do anything to him." God showed great love and concern for Abraham's only son. The heart of God still speaks to us today and calls us to show great love and concern for the weakest members of the human family. The heart of God demands that we take care of our children and do nothing to harm their mental, emotional, spiritual, and physical well-being. The heart of God challenges us anew to do whatever we can to put an end to the exploitation of innocent children. The heart of God illuminates our obligation to do more to protect all children regardless of their race, culture, religious tradition, and social condition. All children are signs of God's presence among us. We are the heart of God empowered by the Spirit to advocate for the weak and powerless and to show great love and concern for children everywhere.

Ponder: How do I reveal the heart of God in the world?

Prayer: Lord, you watch over me and love me as your child. Help me to see all people as your children and treat them with gentleness, love, and respect.

Practice: Today I will pray for gentleness of heart; I will fast from hurtful thoughts and behavior; I will be a good role model for children and youth.

YEAR C

Genesis 15:5–12, 17–18
Psalm 27:1, 7–8, 8–9, 13–14
Philippians 3:17—4:1
Luke 9:28b–36

Jesus took with him Peter and John and James, and went up on the mountain to pray.

LUKE 9:28

Reflection: We get so caught up in our own lives that we seldom think about Jesus' intention to be with us in a quiet place for prayer. Peter and John and James did not realize the gift that Jesus was offering when he invited them to go up the mountain to pray. Prayer is the gift Jesus offers us to be in communion with God and with one another. Prayer is the gift that opens our eyes to see more clearly God's plan for our lives. Prayer is the gift that awakens the heart's desire to be one with God, to live in peace and harmony with all of creation and with all people. Prayer is the gift that grounds us and inspires is to live in faith, hope, and love. Prayer is the gift we offer others in times of their personal suffering, pain, and tragedy. Prayer is a way of keeping things together when the forces of life pull us apart, creating chaos and confusion around us.

Jesus took Peter and James and John up the mountain to teach them that prayer is like climbing up the rough side of the mountain. Prayer is the steady, persistent spiritual work that helps us to remain with the triune God.

Ponder: Do I make time to be with God in prayer?

Prayer: Lord, you desire to be with me and walk with me along life's journey. Awaken in my heart a desire and commitment to be with you in prayer.

Practice: Today I will pray for a spirit of commitment; I will fast from laziness; I will find a quiet place to be with God to pray for the poor.

Second Week of Lent

MONDAY

Daniel 9:4b–10
Psalm 79:8, 9, 11, 13
Luke 6:36–38

[Jesus looked up at his disciples and said:]
"Be merciful, just as your Father is merciful."

LUKE 6:36

Reflection: Within mercy is contained the quality of compassion. Compassion is our ability to feel and identify with another's suffering, and to do our best to alleviate that suffering.

While acknowledging the right of others to experience life in their own way, we can still do our part to alleviate suffering in the world. We can listen to someone in pain without feeling compelled to jump in and find a solution. We can share our own experiences of suffering. We can offer comfort with our words, prayers, and presence.

Caring about others is a sign of our commitment to love our neighbors. Helping with hospice care, participating in a Habitat for Humanity home building project, or taking part in a blood drive are signs of our compassion for our neighbors. Paying fair wages, supporting businesses that treat workers fairly, and exercising our right to vote are further signs of compassion.

We can extend our compassion to all of creation by conserving water, driving less, owning fewer electronic gadgets, planting a garden, and supporting organic and local food growers. We can support agencies that work to prevent cruelty to animals.

Compassion brings awareness that the choices we make have an impact on the lives of others and on our world. Compassion leads us beyond the limits of selfishness to the limitlessness of unconditional love.

Ponder: How do I embody compassion?

Prayer: Lord, you are compassion and forgiveness. Teach me your ways that I may be compassionate as you are compassionate. Show me how to walk gently with my suffering brothers and sisters.

Practice: Today I will pray for a compassionate heart; I will fast from selfishness; I will walk instead of drive.

Second Week of Lent

TUESDAY

Isaiah 1:10, 16–20
Psalm 50:8–9, 16bc–17, 21, 23
Matthew 23:1–12

[Jesus said:] "The greatest among you will be your servant."

MATTHEW 23:11

Reflection: We tend to admire the wealthy, the stars, the politically powerful, and the business tycoons. We tend to define success by how much money a person has, the houses and cars a person owns, the appearances a person makes on television, or the bottom line of a business at the end of the quarter. Yet the definition of success that Jesus has given us is quite different. To succeed in life we are to humbly serve others.

Serving others is not about broadcasting our good deeds or having our name in the church bulletin or winning an award at a banquet. Serving others means bringing a loving presence to those we encounter as we go about our daily activities.

Our world relies on the simple loving acts of ordinary people. Friends who show up at a loved one's wake. Bank tellers who walk an elderly customer to the car. Adults who bend down to tie a child's shoe. Store clerks who walk us right to the product we're looking for. People who take time to understand what we need and do their best to help us. When we make humble service a daily practice, we are sharing our faith in the dignity of all people; we are building up people's hope in goodness; and we are spreading the love of God wherever we go.

Ponder: Am I a humble servant to others?

Prayer: Lord, you teach us to love with all our being and to serve those in need. Open my eyes to see how I may lovingly serve those I meet today.

Practice: Today I will pray for the willingness to serve my brothers and sisters; I will fast from seeking honor; I will practice what I preach.

Second Week of Lent

WEDNESDAY

Jeremiah 18:18–20
Psalm 31:5–6, 14, 15–16
Matthew 20:17–28

[Jesus said:] "Whoever wishes to be great among you must be your servant."

MATTHEW 20:26

Reflection: It is very human to wish to be great, to want recognition. We are so very worried that our lives are unimportant, that what we do means nothing, that we have no real purpose in life. And so we look outside ourselves for appreciation and praise. We become dependent on the opinions of others. We plot ways to be around people of influence and power. We lose our sense of who we really are because we are so caught up with being who we think others will admire. Even the very service we offer others may have an underlying motive of wanting to be noticed or rewarded.

True service is not born from scheming or plotting or wanting to make an impression. It is an impulse of love from our hearts. We notice that someone is in need and, out of compassion, we help. We aren't thinking of a reward. Sometimes, in fact, we're thinking that we're too tired. Yet we move through the resistance and self-centeredness and reach out with the comforting hand, the cheerful smile, the empathetic ear. When we live from our hearts, we are less interested in what others think of us than in how we can better do God's will to love one another.

Ponder: Do I aspire to serve?

Prayer: Lord, your steadfast love guides me at every moment. Help me to know the joy that comes from following my heart and helping those in need.

Practice: Today I will pray to live from my heart; I will fast from needing recognition; I will look for an opportunity to serve someone I meet in my daily rounds.

Second Week of Lent

THURSDAY

_____

Jeremiah 17:5–10
Psalm 1:1–2, 3, 4, 6
Luke 16:19–31

[Jesus said to the Pharisees:] "There was a rich man who was dressed in purple and fine linen and who feasted sumptuously every day. And at his gate lay a poor man named Lazarus, covered with sores, who longed to satisfy his hunger with what fell from the rich man's table."

LUKE 16:19–21

Reflection: We live sumptuously. We have more clothes than we can wear. We eat more food than we need. We live in comfortable homes with heat and clean, running water. We own cars, boats, bicycles, iPods, laptops, televisions, cell phones. We have access to quality medical and dental care. We have public education for all our children.

It is not sinful to enjoy the good things of life. But it is sinful to be indifferent to the needs of those who live without the basic necessities of life. When we ignore the poor, we alienate ourselves from our true nature of goodness and love. We forget to love our neighbors as ourselves. Because we have cut ourselves off from the joy of sharing God's abundance with others, we experience loneliness, dissatisfaction, and restlessness.

It is not difficult to replace indifference with love, compassion, and generosity. It is a simple matter of breaking old habits and learning to share our time, talent, and good fortune with those who have nothing. With this new approach to life, we will experience peace, satisfaction, and serenity.

Ponder: Am I like the rich man?

Prayer: Lord, my hope is in you. Take away my indifference to the poor and suffering. Help me to become a source of hope and healing for all those who are in need.

Practice: Today I will pray for a generous heart; I will fast from indifference; I will make a donation to a local food pantry.

Second Week of Lent

FRIDAY

—

Genesis 37:3–4, 12–13a, 17b–28a
Psalm 105:16–17, 18–19, 20–21
Matthew 21:33–43, 45–46

But when [Joseph's] brothers saw that their father loved him more than all his brothers, they hated him, and could not speak peaceably to him.

GENESIS 37:4

Reflection: Envy springs from feeling inadequate, unlovable, and unsuccessful. Instead of facing these crippling feelings with compassion, we turn them into envy and resentment of others, or bitterness at our lot in life.

When we have the courage to confront envy and resentment, we realize that we have somehow lost sight of how precious we are. We have learned a false lesson that we are a bother, unwanted, and will never amount to anything. We have interpreted words or gestures to mean that we are unacceptable and no one will ever love us. Part of our work in rooting out envy is affirming that we are God's beloved children, that every day our lives have meaning, and that we are lovable just the way we are.

As we learn to replace old negative ways of thinking, we begin to heal. We begin to feel compassion for ourselves, to speak kindly to ourselves, to treat ourselves with respect, and to identify our gifts and talents. We begin to love ourselves.

From this place of self-love, we come to see others as children of God, beloved equally, blessed with different talents and ways of life, but no better or worse than we are. We find the courage to let go of envy and live freely from a spacious heart.

Ponder: Am I hiding behind envy?

Prayer: Lord, you have made us all in your marvelous image of goodness and love. Help me to recognize your goodness in others.

Practice: Today I will pray for the humility to heal from the wounds of self-hatred; I will fast from envy; I will congratulate someone on an achievement.

Second Week of Lent

SATURDAY

Micah 7:14–15, 18–20
Psalm 103: 1–2, 3–4, 9–10, 11–12
Luke 15:1–3, 11–32

Who is a God like you, pardoning iniquity and passing over the transgression of the remnant of your possession? He does not retain his anger forever, because he delights in showing clemency.

MICAH 7:18

Reflection: How blessed are we to know a God who is compassionate, forgiving, merciful, kind, and who delights in showing unconditional love to us all. When we are fully aware of this awesome God in our midst, we cannot help but be moved to a change of heart and humble gratitude.

Who else but God could reach out in comfort when a loved one dies? Who else could forgive the infidelity of a spouse? Who else could feel compassion for a family member who lies and steals to support an addiction? Who else could show kindness to a homeless stranger? Who else could delight in the antics of an adolescent?

In an uncaring, unforgiving, cold, and indifferent world, we can imitate God's compassion, forgiveness, mercy, kindness, and delight. We can be the face and hands of God in our homes, workplaces, communities, and world. We can affirm the presence of a loving God by our willingness to be God-like in our relations with all people, especially those we have rejected, ignored, or despised.

Ponder: When have I experienced the kindness and compassion of God?

Prayer: Lord, you are kind and merciful. Teach me to be slow to anger, quick to forgive, and ready to help my sisters and brothers in need.

Practice: Today I will pray for a spirit of compassion; I will fast from anger; I will treat a stranger with kindness.

Third Sunday of Lent

YEAR A

Exodus 17:3–7
Psalm 95:1–2, 6–7, 8–9
Romans 5:1–2, 5–8
John 4:5–42

The Samaritan woman said to [Jesus], "How is it that you, a Jew, ask a drink of me, a woman of Samaria?"

JOHN 4:9

Reflection: The hostility between Jews and Samaritans is no secret. To the Jews, the Samaritans were the descendents of a mixed population. The Jews did everything in their power not to associate with Samaritans because to do so would make them impure. Calling another person a "Samaritan" was considered an attack on the person's dignity.

Conflict and hostility between people of various races, ethnic groups, cultures, religious traditions, and social backgrounds exist in all parts of the world. The need for one segment of humanity to maintain power and control over another group of people is one of the major obstacles to universal peace and justice. When Jesus approached the Samaritan woman and asked her for a drink of water, he was crossing all the boundaries that kept Jews and Samaritans apart. He was teaching us the importance of dialogue and how essential it is for us to see what is common in all people: the dignity of being created in the image and likeness of God. All people share in common the life-giving breath of God. We are endowed with a common dignity, a common love, and a common vocation to bring an end to all forms of hatred, prejudice, racism, and discrimination.

Ponder: Who is the Samaritan in my life?

Prayer: Lord, you created me to be a member of the human family. Empower me to show respect and love to all people regardless of their racial, cultural, religious, and social background.

Practice: Today I will pray for harmony among all people; I will fast from stereotyping people; I will make the effort to dialogue with people from different religious traditions.

YEAR B

Exodus 20:1–17
Psalm 19:8, 9, 10, 11
Corinthians 1:22–25
John 2:13–25

"You shall not make wrongful use of the name of the LORD your God, for the LORD will not acquit anyone who misuses his name."

EXODUS 20:7

Reflection: It is disrespectful to curse and swear at others using the name of God. The habit of cursing and swearing dishonors our relationship with God and shows a lack of care and concern for the Creator. But this commandment is not just about cursing and swearing; it is concerned with the ways in which we use God's name to justify things that are contrary to the ways of God.

Some people misuse God's name to justify killing others. Some people misuse God's name to manipulate and oppress others. Some people misuse God's name and blame God for natural disasters such as earthquakes, hurricanes, and floods. Some people misuse God's name to enforce unjust laws and inflict punishment on others. Some people misuse God's name to keep people in bondage.

Our relationship with God must reflect the God of the Covenant who promised to be faithful to the people, to show love and compassion in times of need, and to be merciful and forgiving. As partners of God's Covenant, we, too, promise to be like God in the world: faithful, loving, compassionate, merciful, and forgiving toward all people. When we speak and behave negatively toward others, we not only misuse the name of God, we also misuse the power and wisdom of God.

Ponder: When do I misuse the name of God?

Prayer: Lord, you instill within me your power and wisdom. Help me to discern more clearly how to use your power and wisdom in service of my brothers and sisters.

Practice: Today I will pray for discernment; I will fast from misusing God's name; I will speak about God in a respectful, reverent manner.

YEAR C

Exodus 3:1–8a, 13–15
Psalm 103:1–2, 3–4, 6–7, 8, 11
Corinthians 10:1–6, 10–12
Luke 13:1–9

"A man had a fig tree planted in his vineyard; and he came looking for fruit on it and found none. So he said to the gardener, 'See here! For three years I have come looking for fruit on this fig tree, and still I find none. Cut it down! Why should it be wasting the soil?'"

Reflection: Through parables Jesus opened the people's minds and hearts to the deeper meaning of the spiritual life. This parable can help us understand that the Christian person is someone who is grounded in the Word of God, whose life is nurtured by meditation and prayer, and who bears the fruit of love, compassion, and peace in the world. The parable serves as a wake-up call to those who have yet to maximize their full potential, their hidden gifts and talents. Every person has been endowed with a unique gift and talent to be used for the common good of all people. The parable urges us not to waste what lies inside us, but to call forth from within us all that is good and noble and to share it with others. The parable also gives us hope and comfort. God is patient and merciful. God gives us the time we need to deepen our knowledge and understanding of the Word of God, to develop our prayer life, and to show kindness and love to others.

Ponder: What does this parable mean to me?

Prayer: Lord, you are patient with me and never withhold your love and mercy from me. Strengthen me with your grace to become fully human, fully alive in the world.

Practice: Today I will pray for mercy; I will fast from impatience; I will seek the help and guidance of a spiritual director.

Third Week of Lent

MONDAY

2 Kings 5:1–15ab
Psalms 42:2, 3; 43:3, 4
Luke 4:24–30

[Naaman's servants said:] "If the prophet had commanded you to do something difficult, would you not have done it?"

2 KINGS 5:13

Reflection: Sometimes we imagine that doing God's will means life will become dreary, dull, and devoid of pleasure. We are afraid of God's will for us because we worry it will be unpleasant, uncomfortable, or difficult. Yet the beauty of our goodness is that we are open to doing God's will even though we may be convinced we are heading down a route of deprivation and martyrdom.

God's will for us is seldom difficult. It is usually as simple as getting up in the morning and finding something to be grateful for. It is as simple as treating others the way we would like to be treated. It is as simple as intentionally showing love to someone. What God asks of us is usually simple acts of kindness and love.

When we get in the habit of asking God to show us what to do and how to do it, we will find the power to face any task. We will find the patience to wait for the right moment to act. We will find the courage to overcome whatever prevents us from believing God wants us to live joyfully, lovingly, and with delight. We will come to understand that God will not ask us to undertake anything that is too difficult for us.

Ponder: What do I find difficult to do?

Prayer: Lord, your love makes all things possible. Bless me with knowledge of your will for me and give me the power to carry it out.

Practice: Today I will pray for a spirit of simplicity; I will fast from making difficulties; I will get in touch with someone who has been ill.

Third Week of Lent

TUESDAY

Daniel 3:25, 34–43
Psalm 25:4–5ab, 6–7bc, 8–9
Matthew 18:21–35

Yet with a contrite heart and a humble spirit may we be accepted, as though it were with burnt offerings of rams and bulls.

DANIEL 3:39

Reflection: God wants nothing from us. God loves us unconditionally and expects nothing in return. The only offering we can make to God is our whole self. But in order to be able to offer God our whole self, we must make an honest examination of ourselves. We honestly admit our fears, weaknesses, and failures. We acknowledge the harm we have done to others. We face the fact that at times we have been unloving and lacking in respect. With a contrite heart, we ask God for healing and forgiveness. We feel the peace of God's mercy and are strengthened to try again.

Our successes, talents, and joys are a part of who we are, too. With a humble spirit we bring these to God as well. We thank God for such abundance. We ask God for the grace to make good use of all of our gifts in service to others, especially those in need. We feel the relief of admitting our dependence on God. We continue our good work, knowing the one who loves us is supporting our every step.

Ponder: Do I have a contrite heart and humble spirit?

Prayer: Lord, guide me in your truth and teach me your ways. Forgive me for the times I have withheld mercy, compassion, and love from my sisters and brothers. Show me how to use the gifts of love and goodness you have created in me.

Practice: Today I will pray for a humble spirit; I will fast from arrogance; I will forgive someone who has hurt me.

Third Week of Lent

WEDNESDAY

Deuteronomy 4:1, 5–9
Psalm 147:12–13, 15–16, 19–20
Matthew 5:17–19

[Moses spoke:] "But take care and watch yourselves closely, so as neither to forget the things that your eyes have seen nor to let them slip from your mind all the days of your life; make them known to your children and your children's children."

DEUTERONOMY 4:9

Reflection: We have the ability to influence so many people: our children, grandchildren, other family, co-workers, friends, and even strangers. Because the way we live has a lasting impact on those with whom we interact, we have the responsibility of making respect, love, and peace known as our way of life.

We make known our commitment to respect by refusing to tolerate bigotry and prejudice, avoiding gossip, speaking courteously, and showing appreciation for others. We make known our commitment to love by listening to what others have to say without judgment, spending attentive time with friends and family, giving away unused clothing, donating food to the hungry, and visiting those who are ill. We make known our commitment to peace by finding ways to communicate harmoniously, practicing nonviolence in word and action, resolving conflicts through dialogue and changed behavior, and making prayer a part of our daily rituals.

By our life example, we make known God's unconditional love as the foundation of our lives and the source of our strength.

Ponder: How do I make people aware of God's presence?

Prayer: Lord, you have blessed us with your goodness and love. Help me to make your kindness and compassion known to all people by my life example. Help me to fulfill your law of love.

Practice: Today I will pray to be an example of love and compassion; I will fast from being a negative influence; I will make known my love for someone by saying, "I love you."

Third Week of Lent

THURSDAY

Jeremiah 7:23–28
Psalm 95:1–2, 6–7, 8–9
Luke 11:14–23

[Jesus] said to them, "Every kingdom divided against itself becomes a desert."

LUKE 11:17

Reflection: We are each a little kingdom made in God's image of goodness and love. Yet sometimes we feel impatient, anxious, overwhelmed, over-burdened, and under-appreciated. We feel negative, depressed, and lonely. We feel that God has abandoned us. We feel that no one cares about us. We feel lost in a spiritual desert.

Any time we feel off-center and out of control, we have become a divided kingdom. This is the time when we must take a deep look inside ourselves to discover the source of the division. Often we are grieving a loss—job, friendship, marriage, our children heading off to college, health, a loved one's death. Grief is complicated. We go through cycles of anger, blame, bargaining, and depression before we let go and accept reality. We need to be especially gentle during times of grieving.

Sometimes we are afraid—of failure, change, letting others down, the consequences of our actions, the future, death. Fear paralyzes us. It is an inability to love ourselves in the moment. When we recognize the fear, we can reassure ourselves of God's unconditional love and pray to be guided by that love.

Once we acknowledge the source of our inner division, we feel reconnected with God, the source of our wholeness, and find our way out of the spiritual desert we have experienced.

Ponder: What divides my inner kingdom?

Prayer: Lord, you speak words of unity and love. Forgive me for not listening. Show me how to live an integrated life of faith, hope, and love.

Practice: Today I will pray for a spirit of wholeness; I will fast from divisiveness; I will join in a community gathering.

Third Week of Lent

FRIDAY

Hosea 14:2–10
Psalm 81:6c–8a, 8bc–9, 10–11ab, 14, 17
Mark 12:28–34

Jesus answered, "The first [commandment] is, 'Hear, O Israel: the Lord our God, the Lord is one; you shall love the Lord your God with all your heart, and with all your soul, and with all your mind, and with all your strength.'"

MARK 12:29-30

Reflection: To love God with our all our heart means we live from the heart-space of love, joy, and peace. We view the world from this place of non-judgment and harmony and create a welcoming space for those in need of acceptance and compassion.

To love God with all our soul means we spend time in prayer and meditation in order to renew and strengthen our relationship with God. As our conscious contact with God improves, we feel the comfort of God's presence in all areas of our lives and express that healing presence in our interactions with others.

To love God with all our mind means we intentionally practice all that God has taught us: to serve others, feed the hungry, clothe the naked, visit the imprisoned, shelter the homeless, forgive our sisters and brothers, and love our enemies.

To love God with all our strength means we expend our energy in making God's vision of love and peace a reality in the world. We find ways to use our gifts and talents so that others may feel and trust God's presence in the world, drawing strength and hope from it.

Ponder: How do I love God?

Prayer: Lord, you love all people freely. Bless me with the wisdom to understand your way of peace and love. Help me to love you with all my heart, soul, mind, and strength.

Practice: Today I will pray for a spirit of love; I will fast from avoiding God; I will help someone in need.

Third Week of Lent

SATURDAY

Hosea 6:1–6
Psalm 51:3–4, 18–19, 20–21ab
Luke 18:9–14

[[Jesus] told this parable:] "Two men went up to the temple to pray, one a Pharisee and the other a tax collector. The Pharisee, standing by himself, was praying thus, 'God, I thank you that I am not like other people: thieves, rogues, adulterers, or even like this tax collector. I fast twice a week; I give a tenth of all my income.' But the tax collector, standing far off, would not even look up to heaven, but was beating his breast and saying, 'God, be merciful to me, a sinner!'"

LUKE 18:10–13

Reflection: We often get caught up in comparing ourselves to others. Sometimes we compare ourselves to our detriment: we are not as beautiful, not as smart, not as rich, not as kind, not as faith-filled, not as compassionate. Sometimes we compare ourselves to our benefit: we do more, give more, pray more, volunteer more, spend more time with our families. Whenever we get busy looking at others to try to define ourselves, however, we are usually at a point of low self-esteem. We think the way others behave will provide us with what we need to feel good about ourselves.

When we let go of comparing ourselves to others and bring the focus back to our own selves, we find our way to self-acceptance. Self-acceptance is a grace-filled experience where we no longer resist reality. In self-acceptance comes the courage to look deeply at our lives and find areas where we need improvement. We humbly call on God's mercy and ask to be shown a new way of being.

Ponder: When do I compare myself to others?

Prayer: Lord, you are good and merciful. In your compassion, heal my need to compare myself to others.

Practice: Today I will pray for humility; I will fast from comparing myself to others; I will do a good deed in secret.

Fourth Sunday of Lent

YEAR A

1 Samuel 16:1b, 6–7, 10–13a
Psalm 23:1–3a, 3b–4, 5, 6
Ephesians 5:8–14
John 9:1–41

**For once you were darkness, but now in the
Lord you are light. Live as children of light—
for the fruit of the light is found in all that is
good and right and true.**

EPHESIANS 5:8–9

Reflection: The Word of God is the foundation
and source of the Christian spiritual life. We cannot make progress in the spiritual life apart from
the Word of God. The Word of God is the heart of
God that fills the world with goodness and love.
The Word of God is the Light that shines in the
darkness of doubt, hatred, and despair, which can
overwhelm the human condition. The Word of

God can change us and help us understand what it means to be a child of God, a child of the Light.

When we read and reflect on the Word of God, we come to see the truth that Jesus is the Son of God who came into the world to save us, to give us a sense of hope and peace. When we allow the Word of God to shape and rule our life, we become light for others. The Word of God teaches us to model Christ in the world by reaching out to the poor, by loving all people rather than judging and condemning them, by forgiving those who have hurt us, by showing compassion to the sick and suffering, and by finding time for solitude and prayer.

Ponder: How can I be a spiritual light and guide for others?

Prayer: Lord, you are the Word of God that shows me what is good, right, and true. Make me a faithful witness to your Word.

Practice: I will pray for right conduct; I will fast from hypocrisy; I will encourage others to do what is right and just.

YEAR B

---

2 Chronicles 36:14–16, 19–23
Psalm 137:1–2, 3, 4–5, 6
Ephesians 2:4–10
John 3:14–21

But those who do what is true come to the light, so that it may be clearly seen that their deeds are done in God.

JOHN 3:21

Reflection: At baptism we entered into communion with God. We became a new creation and children of the light. We were planted in the God zone. As we go through life we realize that our human experiences are not always in the God zone; we forget where we are and abandon our true self. When we remain in the God zone, we remain in a place of unconditional love, goodness, and peace. We must begin each day with the deep awareness of who we are in the God zone. It is our unawareness that causes us to live contrary to our life in and with God. No matter where we are in the world, we need to be God-like and show others the unconditional love, goodness, and peace of God. Everything that we say and do must be a reflection of life in the God zone.

We need to spend more time reflecting on the meaning of our baptism and how it affects our lives. Our daily struggle is to be a new creation in a world that is, at times, uncaring of God's creation, and to be a light of goodness, compassion, and love in the dark places of people's pain and suffering. The spiritual life is rooted in the God zone. The way to remain in the God zone is to read and meditate on the Word of God, pray daily, and show God's love to everyone.

Ponder: What does it feel like to be in the God zone?

Prayer: Lord, you are the source of love, peace, and justice in the world. Help me to live in communion with you and all people.

Practice: I will pray for enlightenment; I will fast from unawareness; I will visit someone I have neglected.

YEAR C

Joshua 5:9a, 10–12
Psalm 34:2–3, 4–5, 6–7
2 Corinthians 5:17–21
Luke 15:1–3, 11–32

But while he was still far off, his father saw him and was filled with compassion; he ran and put his arms around him and kissed him.

LUKE 15:20

Reflection: The sight of the lost and wounded son triggers a feeling from the depth of the father's being. He is filled up with intense compassion for someone he never stopped loving. The whole world is like the son. The whole world needs to be embraced and kissed, healed of all the hunger and poverty, all the hurt and pain. We can imagine God, at this moment, being moved with compassion for this wounded and broken world. We have walked in the son's shoes; we have made mistakes, squandered our gifts and talents, been rejected by others, and lost our way in life.

No matter what our state in life is, God keeps running toward us with a big heart and open arms, filled up with incredible love and compassion for us. If God does this for us, then we must do this for each other. The true test of what it means to be human comes in the face of human pain and suffering, when we are moved in the depths of our being to show compassion without judgment.

We are made in the image of the compassionate God. We are called to be the compassion of God for others. Compassion is the way to peace and justice. Compassion is the true mark of those who desire to live in union with God and neighbor. We must recommit ourselves to the work of compassion and run toward and not away from the poor, the sick and suffering people in the world.

Ponder: How do I live a compassionate life?

Prayer: Lord, you are the face of God's compassion in the world. Give me a compassionate heart to embrace my suffering brothers and sisters.

Practice: I will pray for compassion; I will fast from intolerance; I will show compassion to someone in need.

Fourth Week of Lent

MONDAY

Isaiah 65:17–21
Psalm 30:2, 4, 5–6, 11–12a, 13b
John 4:43–54

The man believed the word that Jesus spoke to him and started on his way.

JOHN 4:50

Reflection: The words Jesus speaks to us are forgiveness, reconciliation, healing, compassion, peace, and love. When we believe these words of Jesus, we have the foundation for building lives that will reflect God's vision of rejoicing, happiness, and delight.

Sometimes we think that God only speaks to men and women behind monastic walls. We think others can be about the work of forgiveness and reconciliation, but we can still hold on to our grudges and grievances. We think that others have the gifts of healing and compassion, but we lack confidence in our ability to show care and concern. We think that peace and love are never going to happen in our lifetime, and our little efforts don't matter at all.

Yet if we truly believe the words of Jesus, we must let go of all defeatist attitudes and embrace the vision of a peace-filled, happy world. We must take responsibility for our part in making the vision a reality by practicing forgiveness, reconciliation, healing, compassion, peace, and love to the best of our ability. We may stumble at times, but we will find that we become more and more skilled at putting what we believe into practice. We will find it easier to let go of hurts, to make amends to those we have injured, to offer healing words and compassion to those in need, to choose peaceful attitudes, and to love without expectations.

Ponder: What words of Jesus touch my heart?

Prayer: Lord, open my heart to believe your word. Guide me as I learn to play my part in creating your vision of peace and love.

Practice: Today I will pray for the courage to practice what I believe; I will fast from disbelief; I will read Isaiah 65:17–21.

Fourth Week of Lent

TUESDAY

Ezekiel 47:1–9, 12
Psalm 46:2–3, 5–6, 8–9
John 5:1–16

**[Jesus] said to him "Do you want to be made
well?" The sick man answered him, "Sir, I have
no one to put me into the pool when the water
is stirred up; and while I am making my way,
someone else steps down ahead of me."**

JOHN 5:6–7

Reflection: It seems to be a common trait in our
society to communicate with hints and innuendoes, hoping that others will read between the
lines and fulfill our needs. Our failure to communicate in a direct manner often indicates that we
have a low sense of self-worth that feeds our fear
of others. We sigh that we're overworked instead of
asking for the help we need. We make excuses for
our inaction instead of assuming personal respon-

sibility. We lie because we're afraid the truth might get us in trouble. We say yes when we want to say no because we don't want to hurt anyone's feelings.

Although Jesus could read between the lines of what the sick man said, most people cannot read our minds. When we fail to be direct in our communication with others, we risk alienating ourselves from others and perpetuating our low sense of self-worth. As we practice being direct in our communication with others, we will develop healthier relationships and increase our self-confidence.

Ponder: How do I communicate with others?

Prayer: Lord, you are my refuge and strength. Heal my fear of speaking from my heart. Help me to express my thoughts with kindness and directness.

Practice: Today I will pray for a healthy sense of self-worth; I will fast from innuendoes; I will say what I mean and mean what I say—but not be mean about it.

Fourth Week of Lent

WEDNESDAY

Isaiah 49:8–15
Psalm 145:8–9, 13cd–14, 17–18
John 5:17–30

For the Lᴏʀᴅ has comforted his people, and will have compassion on his suffering ones.

ISAIAH 49:13

Reflection: God is the source of the compassion and comfort that we receive from and share with others. No matter what our status in society may be, we are all equal in our need for kindness, comfort, and compassion. Whether we are aware of it or not, we all crave a gentle touch, a kind word of encouragement, or a compassionate presence when we are distressed by life experiences or feel overwhelmed by responsibility.

Some of us like to think that we can go on caring for others without taking time to care for ourselves. Some of us believe that others will not be able to survive without our care and concern. We like it when people rely on us, seeking our comfort, care, and strength.

Although we may think we are the source of comfort and compassion, in truth we are the humble vessels of God's comfort and compassion in the world. We must remember that we are limited in our ability to care for and comfort others, but God never suffers from compassion fatigue. God continues to show great love and compassion to those who are suffering and in pain, strengthening each of us so that we may be able to carry out the works of compassion whenever the need arises.

Ponder: How do I balance care for myself with care for others?

Prayer: Lord, you are good to all. Help me to accept and offer comfort when it is appropriate. Help me to remain a humble servant of your love and compassion.

Practice: Today I will pray to be a comforting presence to others; I will fast from self-neglect; I will be more mindful of how I care for myself and others.

Fourth Week of Lent

THURSDAY

Exodus 32:7–14
Psalm 106:19–20, 21, 22, 23
John 5:31–47

[Jesus said:] "But I know that you do not have the love of God in you."

JOHN 5:42

Reflection: Natural disasters, random killings, war, violence toward others, and greed seem proof that love is absent in the world and people just don't care about each other.

It is a source of grief to realize the harm that people do to each other. Yet when we have the love of God in and among us, we know that the best way to deal with grief is to offer each other the comfort of our loving presence. We counteract violence, terror, and war with our own acts of love. We hold those who are suffering in our hearts and pray for God's healing to comfort them. We pray for God's

Spirit of peace to touch our world and heal the wounds that lead people to hurt other people.

With the love of God in us, we dare to look at our own lives and see where we have forgotten our true nature of love and goodness and have harmed others with our words, our indifference, our selfishness, our expectations, and our resentments.

With the love of God in us, we know our lives make a difference. Every day we choose to shine God's love in the world in small ways and make God's presence a reality for even those who cannot believe.

Ponder: How do I convince others of the love of God?

Prayer: Lord, you bear great love for all your people. Let your love flow in and through me that I may be a source of comfort to those who are suffering.

Practice: Today I will pray for a spirit of peace; I will fast from being anxious about the state of the world; I will respond peacefully to all who speak to me.

Fourth Week of Lent

FRIDAY

Wisdom 2:1a, 12–22
Psalm 34:17–18, 19–20, 21, 23
John 7: 1–2, 10, 25–30

The LORD is near to the brokenhearted.

PSALM 34:18

Reflection: Our hearts break when someone we love dies. Our hearts break when someone we love rejects, abandons, or betrays us. Our hearts break when we confront reality and accept that our lives are unmanageable and that we need help.

When our hearts are broken, we feel at our most vulnerable. In this space of vulnerability, all the walls behind which we have hidden our true self of love and goodness disappear. In this space of vulnerability, we are defenseless yet at our most powerful because we are dwelling in reality with no pretenses distorting our perceptions. In this space of vulnerability and truth, we are at our most open to the love of God. Our broken heart has created a space for us to feel the infinite mercy and compassion of God who loves us totally and who will never betray, abandon, reject, or leave us.

Our state of brokenheartedness doesn't last forever. God's healing and the support of those who love us gradually lead us to a place of renewal. We discover that our brokenness has made us more compassionate toward those who are suffering. We find that our experience of vulnerability has given us a greater insight into the needs of others and a greater ability to offer comfort to those in need.

Ponder: What has caused my heart to be broken?

Prayer: Lord, you are near to broken hearts. Teach me to let go of whatever prevents me from living in the truth of your love.

Practice: Today I will pray for an open heart; I will fast from hiding my true self of goodness and love; I will visit someone who is grieving a loss.

Fourth Week of Lent

SATURDAY

Jeremiah 11:18–20
Psalm 7:2–3, 9bc–10, 11–12
John 7:40–53

[Nicodemus asked,] "Our law does not judge people without first giving them a hearing to find out what they are doing, does it?"

JOHN 7:51

Reflection: Our U.S. civil law has been based on the premise that a person is innocent until proven guilty. Yet do we tend to believe the gossip we hear? Do we tend to perpetuate the prejudices our families have held? Do we tend to accuse immigrants, the unemployed, and the poor of taking advantage of our tax dollars? Do we tend to condemn a whole nation based on the actions of a few people of that nation?

The spirit of our civil law is that we offer all people of every walk of life the chance to explain themselves with an appropriate defender. The spirit of God's law is that we love our neighbor as ourselves, that we love our enemies, that we forgive seventy times seven times, and that we reconcile ourselves with all of our brothers and sisters before approaching the altar of the Lord.

Few of us have led blameless lives. We know that we have caused harm with our words and behaviors. All of us hope for a chance to explain ourselves, to make amends, and to make a new start. All of us wish for someone who will listen and see into our hearts, who will know that we are fundamentally good, and who will speak out on our behalf. All of us have the need to pray for understanding, mercy, and forgiveness.

Ponder: When do I practice the letter of the law versus the spirit of the law?

Prayer: Lord, you search my mind and heart. Heal me of my tendency to judge others unfairly.

Practice: Today I will pray to listen to all sides of an issue; I will fast from condemning anyone; I will ask forgiveness of someone I have hurt.

Fifth Sunday of Lent

YEAR A

Ezekiel 37:12–14
Psalm 130:1–2, 3–4, 5–6, 7–8
Romans 8:8–11
John 11:1–45

"I will put my spirit within you, and you shall live…"

EZEKIEL 37:14A

Reflection: Sometimes we feel like an empty vessel. We feel barren and depleted of all life inside. People come to us looking for love, support, and encouragement, but we think we have absolutely nothing to share. We lack the desire and capacity to care about ourselves and others. We are mentally, emotionally, physically, and spiritually paralyzed. We are spiritless and lifeless.

When we find ourselves slipping into this state of apathy, we need to remember what God has buried inside us, in the depths of our being. We carry within our bodies the life and spirit of God that never runs dry. The life and spirit of God unite us together as a human family. We have an obligation to cherish what God has given us and to care for each other in times of need. The life and spirit of God within us are intended to move our hearts to share the love and compassion of God with others.

In every situation and in every encounter we have with another person, there is an opportunity to share the love and compassion of God. When we lose our desire and capacity to share God's love and compassion with the poor, abandoned, and neglected, people will continue to suffer and die. When we restore our trust in the power of God's love and compassion, the attacks against life will decrease, and human conflicts will end in peace.

Ponder: Who or what empowers my life?

Prayer: Lord, your life-giving spirit fills me with hope and joy. In times of trouble, help me place all my trust in you.

Practice: I will pray for a spirit of hope; I will fast from apathy; I will be more hopeful, loving, and compassionate to the people around me.

YEAR B

Jeremiah 31:31–34
Psalm 51:3–4, 12–13, 14–15
Hebrews 5:7–9
John 12:20–33

I will put my law within them, and I will write it on their hearts; and I will be their God, and they shall be my people.

JEREMIAH 31:33B

Reflection: One of the fastest ways to get a message to someone, share a thought or idea is by text messaging. It is amazing how many text messages are sent each day, connecting people and updating them on a variety of personal, social, and business interests. Text messaging eliminates the interpersonal encounter, removing the components of emotional involvement and physical presence.

In a sense, God text messaged us when the law of God, the law of love, was written on our hearts. Unlike the text messages that flood our cell phones, we cannot erase God's love from our hearts. This is God's permanent law that permeates our mind, heart, soul, and interaction with others. Our thoughts must be inspired with this love. Our spirituality must reflect the spirit of God's love. All our relationships in life must be grounded in love of God and love of neighbor.

The truth is that whatever we say and do, people will be able to read the text message that is written on our hearts and know that it is from God. Since every person on this earth has the law of God written on his or her heart, it means that God desires to be in communion with us, to remain faithful to us, and to care for us. God's text message of love is cellular; it is in our DNA. We cannot ignore the fact that our true nature in God is love. This is the message that goes forth to be shared with all of humanity.

Ponder: Do I feel and act upon the love of God?

Prayer: Lord, your love is written on my heart. May your love inspire and empower me to love people from all walks of life.

Practice: I will pray for a spirit of love; I will fast from hatred of others; I will make an effort to overcome my prejudice of others.

YEAR C

Isaiah 43:16–21
Psalm 126:1–2, 2–3, 4–5, 6
Philippians 3:8–14
John 8:1–11

Do not remember the former things, or consider the things of old. I am about to do a new thing; now it springs forth, do you not perceive it? I will make a way in the wilderness and rivers in the desert.

ISAIAH 43:18–19

Reflection: We allow the past to control us and hold us hostage. We are prisoners within our own mind. We cannot move forward in life as long as we are cemented in the past. We cannot see the good in ourselves if we only remember the bad things we have done in life. We cannot know the joy of life when we are still grieving our losses. We cannot appreciate the gift of life when we keep reopening our emotional wounds. We will never be able to taste the sweetness of success if we only dwell on our mistakes. We cannot know the unconditional love of God if we hold on to the sins of the past.

The present moment in which we stand is a gift from God. In this moment, God desires to do a new thing in us, to help us change and flourish in life. God does not dwell on the past. God awakens in our hearts newness of life with endless possibilities for personal fulfillment and joy. In the wilderness of life, God brings forth rivers of grace, love, and hope. Life looks better and feels better looking ahead, knowing that God works marvelous new things within us. The past cannot become the center of our lives. We must remember that God is the wellspring of our lives. God wants us to be free to become fully human, fully alive.

Ponder: What do I need to let go of from my past?

Prayer: Lord, your grace and love make me whole. Help me to trust in the endless possibilities of the present moment.

Practice: I will pray for a spirit of surrender; I will fast from living in the past; I will prepare for and take advantage of the sacrament of reconciliation.

Fifth Week of Lent

MONDAY

Daniel 13:1–9, 15–17, 19–30, 33–62
Psalm 23:1–3a, 3b–4, 5, 6
John 8:1–11 (Year C: John 8:12–20)

Then the whole assembly raised a great shout and blessed God, who saves those who hope in him.

DANIEL 13:60

Reflection: Some of us feel that our religion is what brings order to our world. We have certain religious tenets we abide by—believing in one God, honoring our father and mother, refraining from murdering, committing adultery, stealing, lying, or coveting others' possessions. We faithfully attend Mass, go to confession, and baptize our children. Our adherence to these rituals helps give meaning to our lives.

Some of us want a living, active relationship with God that goes beyond conforming to religious tenets and receiving sacraments at defined times. We want the spiritual experience of feeling God's presence in our every thought, word, and action. We feel the need to raise a great shout and praise God with our lives.

One way to enhance our conscious contact with God is by reading sacred Scripture. As we spend time with the Word of God, we begin to live with the mind and heart of Jesus, the one who serves, who understands our human suffering and our longing to be with God, who shows us how to love our enemies, forgive our sisters and brothers, and enjoy the company of the poor, alienated, abandoned, and rejected. We begin to reflect the deep love of God in our lives, to express our hope in God's love and compassion, and to pass this hope on to others.

Ponder: In what ways do I praise God?

Prayer: Lord, your goodness and kindness follow me all the days of my life. Help me to shout your praise with every cell of my being.

Practice: Today I will pray for a spirit of hope; I will fast from joylessness; I will read the twenty-third Psalm.

Fifth Week of Lent

TUESDAY

Numbers 21:4–9
Psalm 102:2–3, 16–18, 19–21
John 8:21–30

The people became impatient on the way.

NUMBERS 21:4

Reflection: We express impatience in many ways. Sometimes we are overeager—maybe we can't wait to find out what presents we are receiving for Christmas and we sneak around to find out. Sometimes we express impatience in our intolerance of others—maybe we find others to be too slow to do a task we could do easily ourselves and we criticize their performance. Sometimes we express impatience in anxiety—maybe we have to wait for medical test results and we make ourselves ill worrying about them. Sometimes we express impatience with annoyance—maybe we want immediate gratification for our needs and become exasperated when we have to wait.

Impatience springs from self-centeredness. We think the world revolves around us and our personal needs. We want immediate satisfaction and we try to control the lives of the people around us in order to have our needs met. We have lost sight of God, our true center.

When we live with God at our center, we learn to pray for what we need and leave the outcome in God's hands. We come to trust that God will answer our prayers appropriately. We accept that we are powerless to change other people. We recognize that life events are sometimes out of our control. We find the courage to change ourselves so that we are more loving, compassionate, and respectful of others' needs. We become more skilled at practicing patience and discover a new serenity in our lives.

Ponder: When do I express impatience?

Prayer: Lord, when I call on you, you always answer. Grant me the patience to wait for your reply.

Practice: Today I will pray for serenity; I will fast from impatience; I will take time to teach someone a new skill.

Fifth Week of Lent

WEDNESDAY

Daniel 3:14–20, 91–92, 95
Daniel 3:52, 53, 54, 55, 56
John 8:31–42

[Jesus said,] "If you continue in my word, you are truly my disciples; and you will know the truth, and the truth will make you free."

JOHN 8:31-32

Reflection: Fundamentally we are good and kind people. We take good care of our families. We help out in the community and in our parishes. We give our time, talent, and treasure to support various charities. We make a difference in the world by our willingness to lend a helping hand.

Yet by his example, Jesus calls us to live even more deeply in the presence of God. Every day we must intentionally choose words, attitudes, and actions that imitate Jesus. We need to accept responsibility for the choices we make. We need to speak out in defense of the poor, abused, alienated, and rejected. We need to confront the darkness of hostility, prejudice, and war with the light of reconciliation, justice, and peace. We need to challenge those with authority when they are acting contrary to God's law of love and forgiveness.

Taking time by ourselves for prayer and dialogue with God is essential if we wish to continue in the way of Jesus. In the quiet of our meditation, we gradually begin to see the truth of God's unconditional love and become free of the obstacles that prevent us from being wholly committed to the daily work of forgiveness, love, and peace.

Ponder: How do I live as a disciple of Jesus?

Prayer: Lord, you have sent us into the world to help bring about your kingdom of love. Free me to love my sisters and brothers and reach out to those in need.

Practice: Today I will pray for the courage to be a true disciple of Jesus; I will fast from irresponsibility; I will seek a quiet place and be alone with God for five minutes.

Fifth Week of Lent

THURSDAY

Genesis 17:3–9
Psalm 105:4–5, 6–7, 8–9
John 8:51–59

[God spoke to Abraham:] "I have made you the ancestor of a multitude of nations."

GENESIS 17:5

Reflection: Our daily and weekly celebrations of the Word of God include readings from the Old Testament because the roots of our faith go back much further than the lifetime of Jesus. We come from the line of Abraham, and we share a common heritage with our Jewish and Muslim sisters and brothers. Our common heritage encompasses a belief in the one God who created everything, who is revealed to us through sacred Scripture, and who we are to love with all our hearts, minds, souls, and strength.

All families have multiple branches. Sometimes we have never even met all the relatives who have a place in our family. We have no idea what their daily lives are like, what interests them, or what suffering they have endured. Consider that the number of Abraham's descendants is in the billions. We have spiritual connections all over the world, yet we have very little insight into their lives, cultures, and traditions.

When we are tempted to generalize about others based on their religion or race, we need to take time to reflect on what we actually know about these members of God's family. We can keep in mind our common humanity, our common dignity, and our common need for forgiveness, compassion, and love instead of thoughtlessly judging others for being outwardly different from us.

Ponder: How can I get to know my Jewish and Muslim sisters and brothers?

Prayer: Lord, you are the one God. Forgive my lack of vision. Help me to know, love, and serve my sisters and brothers regardless of their faith, race, or lifestyle.

Practice: Today I will pray to see God's face in everyone I meet; I will fast from prejudice; I will learn more about Judaism and Islam.

Fifth Week of Lent

FRIDAY

Jeremiah 20:10–13
Psalm 18:2–3a, 3bc–4, 5–6, 7
John 10:31–42

In my distress I called upon the LORD; to my
God I cried for help. From his temple he heard
my voice, and my cry to him reached his ears.

PSALM 18:6

Reflection: Pain, sorrow, grief, worry, and fear
are sources of distress. Distress can separate us
from our true nature of love and goodness. We are
thrown off center by whatever is upsetting us. We
try to maintain our normal routine, but we find
ourselves easily distracted, unreasonable, and ir-
ritable. We create even more distress by trying to
force a solution that will resolve our difficulty.

When we finally admit that we cannot solve
our problems by ourselves, we are able to let go of
our pride and call upon God for help. We were not

created to be independent. We were created from God's love to share that love and be a vital part of the community of God. Our cry for help is an admission of our dependence on God. It is a letting go of self-centeredness and arrogance. It is a willingness to be shown a new and better way.

God is not bothered by our pleas for help. God always loves and welcomes us. God always listens to us. God always provides a solution for us. Even if we do not perceive an immediate solution to whatever distresses us, we will experience great relief in surrendering our lives to God's tender care. We will find peace when we turn to God with all our needs.

Ponder: What is distressing me?

Prayer: Lord, you are my rock and my strength. Deliver me from the arrogance that prevents me from asking for help.

Practice: Today I will pray for help; I will fast from overconfidence; I will confide in a trusted friend.

Fifth Week of Lent

SATURDAY

Ezekiel 37:21–28
Jeremiah 31:10, 11–12abcd, 13
John 11:45–56

Now the chief priests and the Pharisees had given orders that anyone who knew where Jesus was should let them know, so that they might arrest him.

JOHN 11:57

Reflection: We have no control over what others do or say, but we do not have to be coerced to act in any way that violates our role as an instrument of God's healing and peace in the world. We keep God's covenant whenever we have the courage to say no to dishonesty, injustice, conspiracy, cover-ups, or witch hunts.

When it is a question of keeping our job, marriage, friendships, or place in society, we might be tempted to act contrary to our true nature of love and goodness. Sometimes we might report back to the boss on others' activities; turn a blind eye to a loved one's alcoholism; go along with the gang; give money to a political campaign in return for some kind of recognition or payback. We might give in to temptation out of fear and insecurity. We might give in to temptation out of ambition and greed. Yet whatever the underlying cause may be, the end result is that we are forfeiting our integrity and abandoning our covenant with God.

It is very human to want to please others. We need to keep in mind, however, that each of us has the right and obligation to examine our conscience and decide on the best course of action that reflects most closely God's command to love God, ourselves, and our neighbors.

Ponder: When am I tempted to betray myself?

Prayer: Lord, you have made us for holiness. Show me how to live according to your covenant of love and peace.

Practice: Today I will pray to dwell in truth; I will fast from intimidating others; I will take time to examine my conscience before making decisions.

Palm Sunday of the Lord's Passion

YEAR A

Isaiah 50:4–7
Psalm 22:8–9, 17–18, 19–20, 23–24
Philippians 2:6–11
Matthew 26:14—27:66

I gave my back to those who struck me, and
my cheeks to those who pulled out the beard;
I did not hide my face from insult and spitting.

ISAIAH 50:6

Reflection: There is something inside us that
wants to fight back against the evil, destructive
forces manifest in the cruel and harsh behavior
of others. We react impulsively when our dignity
has been attacked. We want to strike back imme-
diately when someone insults us with nasty words.
We seek revenge when others have betrayed us. We
take justice into our own hands, making ourselves
judge and jury, when we think that others have not
received their just punishment.

And yet, there is the dark side of us that stands by and watches in silence when others are being mocked and ridiculed. We become deaf to the ethnic and racial slurs hurled at others; we become blind to the endless physical abuse and bullying of others. We lack courage and are afraid to speak out against the cruelty, suffering, and violence inflicted on others. The answer to all the human degradation is not more attacks and violence, but rather nonviolence and mutual understanding.

The vision of Isaiah foreshadows an alternative way of being and acting in the world. Christ models this new way of being and acting in the face of insults and a violent death. Jesus upholds his dignity as the Son of God, demonstrating the power of nonviolence, forgiveness, and unconditional love.

Ponder: How do I react when others hurt and insult me?

Prayer: Lord, you are the model of nonviolence and unconditional love. May your example inspire me to be a more loving and forgiving person in life.

Practice: I will pray for a spirit of forgiveness; I will fast from viciousness; I will be nonviolent and forgiving toward others.

YEAR B

Isaiah 50:4–7
Psalm 22:8–9, 17–18, 19–20, 23–24
Philippians 2:6–11
Mark 14:1—15:47

While [Jesus] was at Bethany in the house of Simon the leper, as he sat at the table, a woman came with an alabaster jar of very costly ointment of nard, and she broke open the jar and poured the ointment on his head.

MARK 14:3

Reflection: We have met certain people in life who have shown us what it means to be totally self-giving and selfless, serving the needs of others. There are parents who pour themselves out each day loving and caring for their children. There are teachers who pour themselves out in the classroom teaching their students the value of knowledge, personal responsibility, and study. There are healthcare providers and social workers who pour themselves out caring for people from all walks of life who have mental, emotional, and physical needs. There are police officers, firefighters, and other civil servants who pour themselves out defending and protecting the lives of others. There are missionaries—clergy, religious men and women, and lay volunteers— who pour themselves out serving the poorest of the poor in underdeveloped countries throughout the world. There are people all over this world who quietly, humbly pour themselves out in caring, loving, compassionate ways without counting the mental, emotional, spiritual, and physical cost. These are the people who show up every day, with their weaknesses and strengths, and open up their loving and compassionate hearts in service to anyone regardless of the person's status and the nature of the need.

Ponder: How do I pour myself out in service to others?

Prayer: Lord, you empty yourself out in loving service to all people. Give me a selfless spirit that I may be of service to others.

Practice: I will pray for a generous spirit; I will fast from hardheartedness; I will give of myself to some work of charity.

YEAR C

Isaiah 50:4–7
Psalm 22:8–9, 17–18, 19–20, 23–24
Philippians 2:6–11
Luke 22:14—23:56

**"Lord, should we strike with the sword?"
Then one of them struck the slave of the high
priest and cut off his right ear. But Jesus said,
"No more of this!" And he touched his ear and
healed him.**

LUKE 22:49B–51

Reflection: We know from this episode at the
Mount of Olives that Jesus spoke out against violence. This was one of the most important teach-
ings of Jesus throughout his ministry. He was the
embodiment of divine compassion and his attitude
of nonviolence was an expression of compassion.
Our children and youth grow up in a world filled
with conflict, violence, and war. Some of them witness acts of violence at home, at school, and in the
streets. They are fed a steady stream of violence
through movies and video games. They think that

violence is a way of life; they believe it is a way to resolve problems. The truth is: violence leads to more violence, and people get hurt in the process.

As Christians we are called to be Christ-like in our relations with others. We betray the God of compassion and Jesus' message of nonviolence when we fail to speak out against domestic violence, child abuse, gang violence in the streets, cyber-bullying, and violence in the workplace. The message of nonviolence must become the message of Christians everywhere. This message has the power to change the minds and hearts of people. As followers of Jesus, we can and must do more to end violence in our society and throughout the world.

Ponder: What have I done to end violence in the world?

Prayer: Lord, your life teaches the way of peace and nonviolence. Help me to imitate your example in times of conflict.

Practice: Today I will pray for patience and understanding; I will fast from provoking others; I will not argue and fight with others.

Holy Week

MONDAY

Isaiah 42:1–7
Psalm 27:1, 2, 3, 13–14
John 12:1–11

You always have the poor with you, but you do not always have me.

JOHN 12:8

Reflection: When we go food shopping, we need to remember that the poor are always with us. When we are having dinner at a restaurant, we need to remember that the poor are always with us. When we are at our favorite store shopping for new clothes or shoes, we need to remember that the poor are always with us. When we are making plans for a vacation trip, we need to remember that the poor are always with us. When we fill the car with gas or get the car washed, we need to remember that the poor are always with us. When we spend money for things we really don't need, we need to remember that the poor are always with us.

Our chronic state of unawareness increases global poverty. Our narcissism keeps us emotionally detached from the poor. Our selfishness makes us numb to the suffering of the poor. Our indifference causes people to starve to death each day. Before Jesus died on the cross, he left his disciples with the unforgettable image of the poor, indicating his solidarity with the poor and concern for their welfare. Every 3.6 seconds, a person dies of starvation. This fact alone ought to be enough for us to turn our gaze to the poor, to stir within us a sense of urgency, and move us to action to respond to the poor.

Ponder: What am I doing to respond to the suffering caused by global poverty?

Prayer: Lord, you are one in solidarity with the poor. Open my eyes to the suffering of the poor and give me the willpower to make a difference.

Practice: Today I will pray for compassion; I will fast from unconcern; I will do one thing to address global poverty.

Holy Week

TUESDAY

Isaiah 49:1–6
Psalm 71:1–2, 3–4a, 5ab–6ab, 15, 17
John 13:21–33, 36–38

"Very truly, I tell you, one of you will betray me."

JOHN 13:21B

Reflection: We know the experience of betrayal. We know the experience of being betrayed by a family member, a close friend, a spouse, a coach, a teacher, a spiritual leader, a coworker, or a business partner. We know what it feels like when someone betrays us. We may feel heartbroken. We may feel unbearable grief or sorrow in the depth of our being. We may feel disbelief. We may feel deep hurt and pain. We may feel deep anger and resentment. We may feel speechless. We may feel empty and numb inside. We may feel the need to be all alone for a while.

There are no words to describe the experience and feelings of betrayal. What we do know is that betrayal leaves us mentally confused, emotionally broken, spiritually wounded, and physically weakened for a long time. We are literally shaken to the core. We disappear when we are betrayed. Our heart stops feeling when we are betrayed. Our spirit evaporates when we are betrayed. We experience a death-before-death when we are betrayed. To be betrayed over and over again is incomprehensible, and yet, this is what Jesus experienced during his life on earth.

Compassion is one of the gifts that God shares with us during Holy Week. It comes to us in the dark experience of betrayal. When we have been betrayed and feel sad, alone, and angry, we need to remember that the God of compassion is with us.

Ponder: When have I been betrayed and when have I betrayed others?

Prayer: Lord, you never turn your back on your own. Help me to remain faithful to myself in times of trouble.

Practice: Today I will pray for a spirit of faithfulness; I will fast from bitterness; I will forgive those who have betrayed me.

Holy Week

WEDNESDAY

Isaiah 50:4–9a
Psalm 69:8–10, 21–22, 31, 33–34
Matthew 26:14–25

The LORD God helps me; therefore I have not been disgraced; therefore I have set my face like flint, and I know that I shall not be put to shame; he who vindicates me is near.

ISAIAH 50:7–8

Reflection: To be the subject of constant criticism, insults, and personal attacks on our character diminishes our sense of self-worth. Being told by others that we are not smart enough, that we don't have the right look, and that we are not good enough discourages us from moving on in life. We feel brokenhearted and humiliated when people reject us because of our language, our culture, our racial or ethnic background, our religious tradition, or social customs. We wake up each day hoping to be accepted by others, only to be ignored and turned away. We try hard to push away the insulting remarks; we pretend that the personal attacks don't hurt. We give the appearance that we are strong and that nothing can destroy us. Deep inside we are in pain and feel ashamed. We look for a friend, an advocate, someone to come to our rescue, and no one is there. We are left alone to deal with our pain.

When we reach our breaking points in life, the grace of God comes to strengthen us and to rescue us. Our faith in God is restored. We believe in our hearts that God helps us and will not let us be put to shame.

Ponder: To whom do I talk when I feel humiliated and rejected by others?

Prayer: Lord, you are near to those who are rejected and brokenhearted. Give me the grace not to give up when others insult me and tear me down.

Practice: Today I will pray for perseverance; I will fast from criticizing others; I will not be cruel or mean to others.

Holy Thursday

Exodus 12:1–8, 11–14
Psalm 116:12–13, 15–16bc, 17–18
1 Corinthians 11:23–26
John 13:1–15

"So if I, your Lord and Teacher, have washed your feet, you also ought to wash one another's feet. For I have set you an example, that you also should do as I have done to you."

JOHN 13:14–15

Reflection: Jesus never asked his disciples how much money they had; he just washed their feet. Jesus never asked his disciples the color of their skin; he just washed their feet. Jesus never asked his disciples what kind of house they lived in; he just washed their feet. Jesus never asked his disciples what their academic backgrounds were; he just washed their feet. Jesus never asked his disciples about their leadership skills; he just washed their feet. Jesus never asked his disciples how many languages they spoke; he just washed their feet.

Washing feet was an act of communion and solidarity. Washing feet was an expression of love and humility. Washing feet was a sign of deep commitment and service. Washing feet was about equality and working together.

Actions always speak louder than words. Perhaps this is why Jesus did not ask any questions and say too many words. Jesus knew that the only way his disciples would understand the meaning of servant leadership was to show them, to give them an example. The only way people will understand what it means to be a disciple of Jesus is not by questioning them but by serving them in a loving, humble, and compassionate way.

Ponder: What kind of disciple am I in the community?

Prayer: Lord, you are the loving, humble servant of God. Give me the grace to be loving and humble like you in the world.

Practice: Today I will pray for humility; I will fast from pride; I will attend the Mass of the Lord's Supper at my parish and pray for the sick.

Good Friday

Isaiah 52:13—53:12
Psalm 31:2, 6, 12–13, 15–16, 17, 25
Hebrews 4:14–16; 5:7–9
John 18:1—19:42

Meanwhile, standing near the cross of Jesus were his mother, and his mother's sister, Mary the wife of Clopas, and Mary Magdalene.

JOHN 19:25

Reflection: The cross is a symbol of punishment, suffering, and death. In the world there is so much punishment, suffering, and death. Innocent people are punished for crimes they never committed; people suffer from disease and famine, cancer, a broken relationship, the loss of a job, or depression. Each day people die as a result of human cruelty, war, and violence. The cross is near us in many shapes and forms.

The women "standing near the cross of Jesus" teach us how to remain faithful in the face of human suffering and hardship. We are all tempted to deny our personal pain and run away from the suffering of others. The women show us what true love and compassion look like. At certain moments of life, we are called to keep vigil with those who are suffering and in pain. We are invited to participate in their anxiety, struggle, and weakness. Being present with them is our gift of love and compassion.

As members of the Body of Christ, we must keep vigil with those who bear the cross of suffering and pain. The women take us to the cross of Jesus and invite us to enter more deeply into the mystery of the life and death of Jesus. Their witness of faith, love, and compassion teaches us how to give hope and strength to others in times of suffering.

Ponder: How do I respond to the pain and suffering of others?

Prayer: Lord, you showed the depth of your love by accepting suffering and death on the cross. Give me the grace to follow in your footsteps.

Practice: Today I will pray for acceptance; I will fast from indecisiveness; I will participate in a Good Friday service and pray for people suffering throughout the world.

Easter Vigil

YEAR A

Genesis 1:1–2:2
Psalm 104:1–2, 5–6, 10, 12, 13–14, 24, 35
Romans 6:3–11
Matthew 28:1–10

After the Sabbath, as the first day of the week was dawning, Mary Magdalene and the other Mary went to see the tomb.

MATTHEW 28:1

Reflection: It is not the tomb that calls us but the power of love. In the days following the death of a loved one, some people return to the grave site to keep vigil or to keep watch over their deceased family member, relative, or friend. The overwhelming sense of sadness and grief gives way to prayer, conversation, and periods of silence. The pain of loss is intense because the love is so deep.

With love in their hearts, Mary Magdalene and the other Mary went to the tomb with a question:

Is it possible to love someone back into existence? Our faith is grounded in the love of God that makes all things new. When the women found the tomb empty, they were convinced that God's love had raised Jesus from the dead. This was the dawn of a new day for them, the disciples, and for all of humanity.

The resurrection of Jesus from the dead is a triumph of love and an affirmation of life. Mary Magdalene and the other Mary represent all those who believe in the promise of eternal life and the power of God's love. The resurrection points us in a new direction beyond the grave, beyond death to new life with God. The unbreakable bond of love that we have with Jesus and our loved ones keeps us seeking for union with God.

Ponder: How has the resurrection changed my life?

Prayer: Lord, your rising from the dead increases my faith, hope, and love. May my belief in your resurrection change my attitude and behavior toward others.

Practice: Today I will pray for a renewed heart; I will rejoice in the gift of life; I will share God's love with all people.

YEAR B

Exodus 14:15—15:1
Exodus 15:1–2, 3–4, 5–6, 17–18
Romans 6:3–11
Mark 16:1–7

"Who will roll away the stone for us from the entrance to the tomb?"

MARK 16:3

Reflection: A stone is a symbol of something that blocks, obstructs, or prevents passage. A blocked artery keeps oxygen-rich blood from flowing into the heart muscle, causing discomfort, shortness of breath, heart disease and failure. Unless the artery is unblocked, the chances of heart failure are increased.

On a spiritual level, the love of God in our hearts is blocked by fear, anger, resentment toward others, jealousy, or selfishness. These are the stones in our hearts that can cause spiritual discomfort and death within us. Left unattended, we project our inner pain and discomfort onto others, inflicting hurt and pain in their lives.

As Christians, we believe that baptism makes us one with the risen Lord who lives in our hearts. Our attitude and behavior toward others is supposed to be a reflection of what is in our hearts. Until the stones of fear, anger, resentment toward others, and selfishness are removed from our hearts, the love of the risen Lord cannot be experienced by others.

At Easter all the stones have been rolled back from the entrance of our hearts so that the love and peace of the risen Jesus can go forth into the world. For believers, the resurrection opens up new ways and opportunities for people to experience the liberating power of God's love.

Ponder: What is blocking my ability to experience the presence of the risen Lord?

Prayer: Lord, your rising from the dead gives the world renewed hope. Remove the obstacles from my life that keep me from believing and trusting in the power of your resurrection.

Practice: Today I will pray for freedom; I will rejoice in the promise of the resurrection; I will open my heart to welcome others with love and peace.

YEAR C

Ezekiel 36:16–17a, 18–28
Psalms 42:3, 5; 43:3, 4
Romans 6:3–11
Luke 24:1–12

"Why do you look for the living among the dead? He is not here, but has risen."

LUKE 24:5B

Reflection: The feast of the Resurrection is not for the dead but for the living. On Easter Sunday, most churches will be packed full with people who are full of life. For some mysterious reason, people come out from hiding; they come from every corner of the earth to be present for the Easter celebration. The regular attendees will be complaining because their seats have been taken by strangers or visitors. This is a perfect day to tell all the people gathered that Jesus has already risen from the dead. It is the perfect opportunity to remind ourselves, our friends, and neighbors that every day we carry within us the power of the resurrection.

The resurrection was never intended to be left in our churches, in our prayer books and hymnals, in the collection basket, at the pulpit, or on the altar. The resurrection was intended to be given to all the living, to be carried out into the world, to all the dark places where people need the reassuring presence of the risen Christ embodied in a caring, loving, compassionate person.

Easter is a beautiful day to ground ourselves in the message and power of the resurrection and recommit ourselves to the endless task of renewing God's creation and a broken, fragile humanity. The living one is not in our churches but in the hearts of all believers.

Ponder: To whom do I bring the presence of the risen Lord?

Prayer: Lord, the power of your resurrection lives in the hearts of all believers. May your resurrection empower me to bring love, hope, and peace to others.

Practice: Today I will pray for renewed faith; I will rejoice in the gift of the resurrection; I will share my understanding of the resurrection with others.

Easter Sunday

YEARS A, B, C

Acts 10:34a, 37–43
Psalm 118:1–2, 16–17, 22–23
Colossians 3:1–4 or 1 Corinthians 5:6b–8
John 20:1–9

Early on the first day of the week, while it was still dark, Mary Magdalene came to the tomb and saw that the stone had been removed from the tomb.

JOHN 20:1

Reflection: We cannot avoid the darkness. We must embrace the darkness of life, the darkness of uncertainty, the darkness of fear and ignorance, the darkness of sadness, the darkness of failure and disillusionment, and the darkness of self-betrayal. We must learn to keep moving through the darkness in the absence of care, love, and compassion.

Mary Magdalene knows her own darkness but does not allow this darkness to engulf her life and keep her from moving forward into the light. She walks through the darkness with hope in her heart. In this darkest moment, she still seeks the one she loves at the tomb. It is this empty tomb that sheds light in her darkness and heightens her desire to be with the Lord.

The resurrection story can help us to make sense of the many shades of darkness in our lives. Mary Magdalene shows us how to walk through the darkness of life with deep trust and faith. The resurrection story reminds us that we live in a world of darkness and light, but that light triumphs over the darkness. Easter reassures all believers that the light of God's love and mercy embodied in the risen Lord triumphs over all the darkness that keeps us sad, unfulfilled, and afraid.

Ponder: What darkness paralyzes me and keeps me afraid?

Prayer: Lord, your resurrection pierces the darkness of doubt and fear. May the power of your resurrection help me to deepen my love for you and all people.

Practice: Today I will pray for perseverance; I will rejoice in the light of your resurrection; I will ask for help to overcome my inner doubt and fear.

Also by the authors

*Joyful Meditations for Every Day of Advent
and the Twelve Days of Christmas*

Other Resources for the Lent and Easter season

*Seven Words of Jesus and Mary
Lessons on Cana and Calvary*

. . . .

*Characters of the Passion
Lessons on Faith and Trust*

. . . .

*The Essential Lenten Handbook
A Daily Companion*

. . . .

*Behold the Cross
Meditations for the Journey of Faith*

. . . .

*Live Lent at Home
Daily Prayers and Activities for Families*

. . . .

*Lent and Easter Wisdom from:
Saint Benedict
Saint Ignatius of Loyola
Saint Francis and Saint Clare of Assisi
Henri J.M. Nouwen
Fulton J. Sheen
Thomas Merton*

*For other books in this series and additional
seasonal resources, please visit your local bookstore
or
www.liguori.org*